You and Your Pet
Kitten

Jean Coppendale

QED Publishing

First published in the UK in 2004 by
QED Publishing
A Quarto Group Company
226 City Road
London, EC1V 2TT

www.qed-publishing.co.uk

A Catalogue record for this book is available from the British Library.

ISBN 1 84538 283 8

Written by Jean Coppendale
Consultant Michaela Miller
Additional contribution by Joanna Oldham
Designed by Susi Martin
Editor Gill Munton
All photographs by Jane Burton
With many thanks to Marianna and James Peet
Picture of Fluffy on page 29 by Georgie Meek
Creative Director Louise Morley
Editorial Manager Jean Coppendale

Printed and bound in China

Words in **bold** are
explained on page 32.

Contents

Your first kitten

It's fun to have a kitten as a pet. Kittens are furry, **purry** and playful, and lovely to stroke and cuddle.

Most cats like to play, but a fully grown cat may not be as cute and playful as a kitten.

◀ **Kittens are not toys. They can be easily hurt, and they should be treated very gently.**

▼ **A kitten needs a lot of looking after and will take up a lot of your time.**

Parent Points

If your child is very active and noisy, or if there are several children living in your home, a kitten is not the best kind of pet. Kittens can be very timid and easily scared. If a kitten is frightened, it can be very difficult to regain its trust.

Kittens look cute, but they grow up.

If you get bored or fed up with your pet, you can't throw it away like a toy. Cats can live for 20 years or more, so your cat may be with you for a very long time.

Which kitten?

Kittens are all different. Some have long hair and some have short hair – and they come in lots of different colours!

◀ **Short-haired kittens like these are easier to look after because they do not need a lot of grooming.**

Long-haired kittens need a lot of grooming.

A tabby kitten

Pedigree kittens, like this Chocolate Point Siamese, are usually only available from a specialist breeder.

Lots of cats

All these cats are pedigree breeds. A pedigree cat has been bred over a long time to have certain features and colours.

▲ Maine Coon

▲ Manx

◀ Siamese

▲ Persian

▲ Ragdoll

◀ Scottish Fold

▲ Rex

▲ Exotic Shorthair

9

Kitten shopping list

Your kitten will need:

▶ **A basket or a box to sleep in with a blanket or a cushion**

▶ **A special spoon or fork – always use this to serve the cat food**

▼ **Two bowls, one for water and one for food, or a double bowl**

◀ **A cat carrier for trips to the vet or the cattery**

▼ **A brush**

▲ **A litter tray and some litter**

▲ **Cat toys – make sure they are not too big or too heavy for a kitten, or so small that your kitten could swallow them**

Your kitten might like some toys.

▲ **A collar for when your kitten is ready to start going outside**

Parent Points

Even if you have a garden, you will need a litter tray for the first 14 weeks. Keep your kitten indoors until it has been fully vaccinated. The first set of vaccinations are normally done when kittens are between 8–12 weeks old and the second set two weeks later. Booster shots must then be given regularly. You may also need to consider installing a cat flap.

Getting ready

◀ **Your kitten will race around and climb up the furniture, so make sure that there are no ornaments or plants that might fall over and get broken or hurt the kitten.**

Make sure that your home is safe for your new kitten.
Have a look around …
are there any electrical wires that your kitten could chew or get tangled up in?

Before you let your kitten explore the garden, make sure that there is a way of finding it if it gets lost.

Your kitten can wear a collar with a name disc, or your vet can give it an **identity chip**.

▲ **If you give your kitten a collar it should not be too tight, and it should have an elastic strip so that the kitten can escape if it gets caught on anything.**

Saying hello

Getting your first kitten is very exciting, but you must be gentle with it. When your kitten arrives in its new home, put it in the room where its bed, food and litter tray are. Leave your kitten in the room to have a look around quietly by itself and get used to its new surroundings. It will explore and get used to all the new smells and noises.

Don't chase your kitten or grab it.
Make sure there is a box for it to
play in, or to hide in if
it gets frightened.

Make a bed for your kitten by
putting a soft cushion in a box,
or show it where its basket is.
Then show your kitten where
its food bowl is, and give
it a little food.

▲ **Your kitten's
bed and its food
bowl should be
somewhere quiet.**

Parent Points
Gently place the
kitten on its litter tray
as soon as it arrives,
but don't force it to sit.

A kitten may spend the
first few days hiding under a
table or behind a cupboard.

Make sure its food is nearby,
but leave it alone to get
used to the change.

Handle with care

When you stroke your kitten, always start from the head and move your hand towards its tail.

Never pat your kitten hard, and never pull its tail or **whiskers**. Do not push or pull your kitten and never squeeze it.

▼ **Tickle your kitten under its chin and scratch its head, but always be gentle.**

◀ **Some kittens like to be cradled but many don't. If your kitten starts to struggle when you pick it up or while you are holding it, put it down straight away.**

When you pick up your kitten, put one hand around its front half and the other hand under its bottom. Don't let its back legs hang down. Never drop your kitten, as it may get hurt.

Parent Points

If your child is very young, make sure that he or she is sitting on a chair or on the floor when holding the kitten, as a sudden movement may make the child drop the kitten.

Make sure the child never holds the kitten too close to his or her face, as it may accidentally scratch the child. Make your child aware that kittens have very sharp claws and teeth.

Looking after your kitten

Cats and kittens like to eat regular meals. Feed your pet in the same spot and at the same time – once in the morning and once in the evening for an adult cat. A kitten needs four to five small meals every day and fresh water to drink.

▲ **Always make sure that your kitten's food bowl is clean.**

Your kitten will need a cosy bed. Make sure that the bed is not in a draughty spot or near a door, or in a place where people move around a lot.

◀ **Put a cushion or a piece of soft blanket in a box, and place it in a quiet corner.**

Always use a special cat brush for your kitten. Brush from the head towards the tail, and don't press too hard.

If you have a long-haired kitten, you should brush it every day. A short-haired kitten should be brushed about once a week. Always use a special cat brush. If your pet has tangled fur, ask an adult to help you brush out any knots and tangles.

You, kitten's life cycle

(5)

▶ At five to six months your kitten will need two to three meals a day.

(4)

1

◀ A newborn kitten cannot see or hear, or stand up.

2

◀ A female cat can have kittens when it is about six months old. New-born kittens drink thcir mother's milk. This is called suckling.

▲ At three weeks old, a kitten can walk and run about and have some solid food.

3

◀ At 10 to 12 weeks a kitten is old enough to leave its mother.

Let's play!

Make a toy for your kitten. If you have an old sock, put a ping-pong ball inside the toe and tie a knot in the sock. Roll this along the floor, and watch what your kitten does.

Always be gentle when you play with your kitten. Never chase it around the house or throw things at it.

Your kitten will enjoy playing with a long piece of string or wool. You could tie a piece of string or wool around a newspaper ball and pull it across the floor.

▲ **Crumple a sheet of paper into a ball, and roll it across the carpet for your kitten to chase.**

Parent Points

If you make toys for your kitten, always watch when your kitten is playing with them – it may try to swallow one. All good quality shop-bought toys are normally safety tested.

Understanding your kitten

When your kitten **purrs**, it usually means that it is happy. But sometimes cats purr when they are nervous or in pain.

When your kitten pushes its **paws** up and down in your lap (kneading), it wants to settle down and go to sleep.

Do not make any sudden movements near your kitten. This will scare it, and it might scratch you.

Kittens have very good hearing, so never shout at your pet, make loud noises near it or put it in a room where very loud music is played.

Talk quietly to your kitten, and it will soon learn to recognize your voice. If you are gentle, your kitten will soon trust you.

Kitten watching

◀ When a kitten has its ears back, it is ready to attack. Keep away.

▲ When a kitten rolls on its back like this, it feels happy and safe.

When a kitten rubs against you, it is leaving its scent and being friendly.

When a kitten puts its bottom in the air like this, it probably wants to play.

When a kitten comes towards you with its tail in the air, it is pleased to see you.

Saying goodbye

Your kitten is growing and getting older all the time – just as you are. As your cat gets older it will sleep more, move more slowly and play less, but it will still enjoy cuddles and strokes.

Many older cats have stiff joints. If this happens to your pet, make sure its food, bed and litter tray are easy to reach.

Fluffy last summer

◀ **If your cat becomes ill, make sure that it is kept warm and quiet.**

Parent Points

A very sick cat may need to be put to sleep. This will need sensitive handling.

If your child's cat dies, let him or her cry and express sadness. Writing a story about the pet – or putting together a scrapbook or montage of photos and drawings – can be very therapeutic.

It's not always a good idea to replace the pet immediately . . . let your child grieve first.

My cat Fluffy

Keep a special scrapbook about your pet.

If your pet is very old or ill, it may die. Try not to be too sad, but remember all the fun you had together.

You may want to bury your pet in the garden, and perhaps grow a special plant or tree where it is buried.

Kitten checklist

Read this list, and think about all the points.

✔ **Kittens are not toys.**

✔ **Kittens and cats have sharp claws and teeth, and may scratch and bite if they are teased or they are scared. If your pet scratche or bites you, don' hit it. Try and think about why i scratched or bit.**

✔ **Cats can live for 20 years or more – will you get bored with your pet?**

✔ **If you care for your kitten properly, it will be a friend for life.**

✔ **Treat your kitten gently – as you would like to be treated yourself.**

✔ **Never hit your pet, shout at it, drop it, chase it or throw things at it.**

✔ **Kittens grow – they don't stay small and cute for ever.**

Parent's checklist

● **You**, not your child, are responsible for the care of the kitten.

● Cats are expensive pets. Work out how much it will cost to feed the kitten and pay the vet's bills. Your vet will give you advice on essential procedures such as annual vaccinations, worming and treatment for fleas.

● You should not leave a cat alone for more than one night. If you go on holiday, who will look after your cat? Is there a willing neighbour who will check on and feed your cat twice a day, every day, or will the cat have to stay in a cattery? Consider the cost of a stay in a cattery – on top of your holiday bill.

● Some cats are more suitable for children than others. Your vet, the breeder or the staff at animal rescue centres will advise you.

● Homes with gardens are ideal for cats – but will you be happy for your kitten to use a flowerbed as a toilet? If it uses a litter tray, make sure your child does not go near it (cat faeces can carry disease), and change the litter every day. Litter trays and regular supplies of litter are an additional cost.

● Never leave a young child and a kitten alone together – they should always be supervised.

● If the kitten scratches your child, bathe the scratch immediately and put antiseptic cream on it. If your child is bitten, phone your local doctor for advice – cat bites can transmit infection.

● Wherever you live, it's sensible to have your kitten neutered – whether it's male or female. Female cats can become pregnant up to three times a year and have five or six kittens in each litter.

Kitten words

Some kittens have **eyebrows**.

The long hairs on a kitten's face are called **whiskers**.

A kitten can **purr** – it makes this sound in its throat.

The sound a kitten makes is called a **miaow**.

Its fur is called a **coat**.

A kitten's feet are called **paws**.

Kittens have sharp **claws**.

If you ask your vet for an **identity chip**, your pet's details will be put on a microchip which the vet inserts under your pet's skin. Vets and animal centres have scanners that 'read' the chip so that lost animals can be returned home.

A **vaccination** is an injection to stop your kitten from catching serious diseases.

Index